*This work is dedicated
to all who yearn for deeper
and more authentic connections
with themselves and others.*

*May your relationships
enrich and fulfill you.*

Contents

How to Use this Study Guide
A Note from the Author
Course Description
Learning Objectives
Course Outline
Workshop Evaluation

What is a Boundary?
Schools of Thought
Important Terms
Disclaimer
Emotional Impoverishment
Types of Boundary Violations
Effects of Growing Up Without Boundaries
Rules for the Co-Dependent Family
My New Rules
Universal Needs
Building Skills
Anatomy of an Emotion
On Conflict
On Guilt
On Forgiveness
Suggested Reading

Appendices

Appendix I Playing The Victim
Appendix II Blame Versus Accountability
Appendix III Developmental Tasks and Skills
Appendix IV The Toxic Trio
Appendix V Conscious Parenting
Appendix VI Negative Assumptions from Childhood
Appendix VII Chaos
Appendix VIII Basic Needs and Limits
Appendix IX Emotions
Appendix X Conflict
Appendix XI Guilt
Appendix XII Forgiveness
Appendix XIII Working Definitions

How to Use this Study Guide

First of all, this is not a self-help book. Its purpose is to serve as a foundation, or a jumping-off point for the learning and application of boundaries as an enhancement to true intimacy; to sharing your authentic self safely with others. It is intended to serve as a companion to the five-week course, *Boundaries 101*, facilitated by the author, Toni Rahman. Contained within this booklet is a collection of excerpts from many great thinkers and many published works. Herein you will be introduced to the ideas necessary in the pursuit of understanding boundaries.

So much of what is contained in this Study Guide is the work of other authors that a special format was necessary to give each one of them adequate credit for their work. A special effort was made to keep the work of other authors true to its original form, while maintaining consistency and flow between authors and schools of thought. Each appendix is an excerpt from a single author. The body of the booklet (prior to the appendices) is largely that of Toni Rahman, Licensed Clinical Social Worker, except when the material is in quotes, or otherwise set off from the material that was written by Toni.

A Note from the Author

I am thrilled to be sharing *Boundaries 101* with you. I hope you walk away from this course with a sense of budding inner strength something akin to a martial art; offering a quiet calm and self-assuredness that sends potential offenders in the opposite direction before you even need to interact with them. Also like a martial art, building boundaries is an ongoing discipline that will require practice, dedication, humility and persistence to master.

Secondly, I would like to encourage you to persist in your learning because it will take more than five weeks to integrate these ideas into your life. Take note of the ideas and authors that you find particularly interesting and helpful, read their works, and continue to learn. This is a worthwhile endeavor and will pay great dividends in terms of your relationships, your life outlook, and your health. I am not exaggerating when I say that recognizing and honoring your personal boundaries will change everything for the better.

Finally, there may be times when the best boundary you can have is physical space. When you are facing abuse, or when the person you are with is out of control, or not behaving responsibly, you are not safe. You *always* have the option of physically removing yourself, whether you give an explanation or not. Never be too proud or principled to leave an abusive situation.

Sometimes just knowing that you can use your feet to set a boundary is all you need.

Praise for Boundaries 101

"The class made me passionate about myself in a different way than before. I am learning that I do not need to be perfect and I should not hold that for others either. I am now finally learning how to say no and it feels so good! I have even learned how to not attack my partner by using victimstance or even trying to be perfect for others to like/accept/admire me. That does not mean that I don't fall off the wagon. Last weekend I started doing victimstance and said, 'hold on, that is victimstance, let me rephrase that.' It will be a constant work in progress, that is for sure, but the vital thing to remember is that I want to constantly be working on this and I strive to not be perfect at boundaries for myself, but start building them!"

W.B., Graduate Student University of Missouri

"In this class, I've been realizing how to be me and value who I am by asking for what I need and respecting myself enough to not allow hurtful things in my life without standing up for me."

S.M., Columbia Public Schools - Educator

"I had a lot of striking moments during class, learning about boundaries, and how my boundaries have been violated in the past, presently, how things have come up, and I noticed myself not seeking approval from others, and telling myself that I am okay, I imagine the protective shield around me when I am anxious or scared, and it helps. Also, the [resources shared during class] really gave me a lot of insight into how to look at my emotions in a subjective, practical way, without overreacting to them. I hope to carry this knowledge with me, and work on exercises to improve on my setting boundaries and continue to grow and get better at setting boundaries for myself."

T.D., Hospital Administrator

Boundaries 101

Learning to Recognize, Honor & Communicate Your Personal Limits

Study Guide

by

Toni Rahman, LCSW

Course Description

Understanding boundaries and how they connect to your emotions is an important part of maintaining healthy relationships. This course is a practical guide geared to provide information and training to people who may have had trouble setting boundaries and recognizing boundary violations in the past, or for people who would just like to strengthen their sense of Self. This five-week course provides education about the nature and implications of boundaries. Using a wide variety of learning tools and activities, Toni creates a forum in which participants practice what they learn in a safe and supportive environment. Participants will leave this course with a full introduction to the connection between self care and boundaries.

Learning Objectives

- Learn what a boundary is, and what its function is.

- Learn the importance of setting and maintaining healthy boundaries.

- Understand emotions and how they are related to boundaries.

- Learn how to set and maintain healthy boundaries.

- Learn to recognize when a boundary is being violated.

- Learn various strategies to protect yourself from manipulation.

- Learn how to honor and respect the boundaries of others.

- Understand the connection between self care and boundaries.

Course Outline

WEEK 1
>Establishing a Safe Environment for Learning
>Introduction to Boundaries
>>What is a boundary?
>>What constitutes a boundary violation?
>>Destructive Control Behaviors

WEEK 2
>What makes people behave this way?
>What can I do about it?
>>Recognizing Needs
>>Recovery of the Self
>>Studying One's Self

WEEK 3
>Emotions Overview
>>Internal World of Emotions
>>External World of Emotions
>The Function of Emotions

WEEK 4
>Communicating Boundaries
>3 Basic Skills
>*Basic Skill #1:* Strengthening the ability to tolerate unpleasant emotions.
>*Basic Skill #2:* Using a pause before responding to the requests of others.
>*Basic Skill #3:* Asking for clarification.
>Identifying and Disabling Emotional Hooks

WEEK 5
>Nurturing Myself
>Building an Inner Authority
>Opening the Possibility for Trust

What is a Boundary?

A boundary is an energetic or otherwise communicable membrane between one person or entity and another. A boundary is what allows me to retain connection with my self and my state of mind, responsibility and business, regardless of your state of mind, responsibility or business. A boundary is what allows me to maintain a degree of safety when I am in the presence of ill, angry, or otherwise unhappy people.

Schools of Thought

Let's face it. Boundaries are a confusing and ill-defined concept. And lack of good boundaries is the source of much pain and suffering in the world. This course is a primer on boundaries, offering a place to explore the anatomy of a boundary, reasons why boundary setting has been difficult for us in the past, and what we can do to set healthy boundaries in the future. It will also provide a forum in which we can dissect specimens of the various boundary violations we encounter in our lives, and a safe place where we can practice new skills, so that we can be better equipped to hold our own in the presence of even the most insidious boundary busters.

Included in this Study Guide are discussions by Clinton S. Clark, who comes from a largely Adult Children of Alcoholics perspective. The final reading in this collection is a comprehensive set of definitions by Clark. Other perspectives I came across during my studies include a layman's guide to avoiding "Emotional Bullshit" by Carl Alasko;" a couple of mental illness perspectives in *Disarming the Narcissist*, by Wendy T. Behary, and *I don't want to talk about it: Overcoming the secret legacy of male depression*, by Terrence Real; *Controlling people*, by Patricia Evans and her other books on verbal abuse; and a couple of early childhood perspectives, including developmental landmarks from the co- and counter-dependency literature by Janae and Barry Weinhold, and the implication of boundaries in adolescence in *Get out of my life but first could you drive me and Cheryl to the mall?* by Anthony E. Wolf, Ph.D. The 12-Step literature is full of less specific but wonderfully supportive material on boundaries. Though I have not included them in this list, I highly recommend anything that is Al-Anon Conference Approved as an invaluable means of scaffolding and support for the journey you are about to embark upon. I have included a reading list at the end of this booklet if you would like to continue your studies after this course.

As you can see, I am drawing upon a broad range of fields where boundaries are relevant. I hope that this reading will give you a sense of respect for the immensity of the topic at hand, and a healthy measure of gentleness for yourself, if you have not yet mastered this skill. You are in good company. Each perspective uses its own set of concepts and its respective terminology, which we will begin to discuss next. If you have not already done so, please complete the Counter-Dependence Checklist that came as an insert with this Study Guide, and bring it to class with you on Week 1.

Important Terms

The topic of boundaries comes up a lot in the context of domestic violence, where two or more people live together, share their lives, and engage in that dangerous dance that so baffles and mystifies us. What one can observe about an abusive relationship, however, is that it is based not upon intimacy and authentic connection, but upon POWER and CONTROL. The dance is about being right, being better, proving a point; the ever-present illusion of getting enough power to somehow affect the other. Here is where it is easy to see the caricatures of the co-dependent and counter-dependent personalities. With the CO-DEPENDENT, we conjure the image of the person who lacks self-confidence, who cannot make a decision on "her" own, and who sacrifices "her" own values and strength for an illusory hope that "she" will be taken care of, and thus places herself in the hands of another. "She" is passive aggressive and prone to manipulative emotional outbursts. With the COUNTER-DEPENDENT, we see the person who cannot allow "his" vulnerabilities to be seen, hates commitment, fears being controlled, and gives the outer impression that "he" has no feelings or compassion. What I'd like to suggest is that these are roles that we assume in relationship when we lack the skills to connect authentically. Neither of these roles is associated with gender, or is even necessarily assigned to a single person. Instead, I'd like for you to look at these roles as coping mechanisms that we assume as the result of developmental delays. Later in this guide we will discuss what happens in the development of a healthy child, and the implications for individuals who have yet to develop still-necessary skills.

For now, let's just say that CO-DEPENDENCY happens when there is an interruption in the bonding process. COUNTER-DEPENDENCY happens when healthy individuation does not take place. Counter-dependency is interesting also in that it is often indirectly related to the failure to adequately bond. So with the counter-dependent person, there is the tendency, in a relationship, to flip-flop from one role to the other.

Use of the word ABUSE in this course is intended in the most broad sense possible. Abuse happens whenever a boundary is violated. Any one of us is capable of breaching another's boundaries. In this course, we will not be punished for this, nor will we be punishing others. We will learn to be more conscious about what abuse looks and feels like, and how the failure to observe and/or communicate about boundaries tears us down as individuals and impedes authentic relating.

During this course, I'd like for you to keep in mind the analogy of a martial art. In this way it may be easier to remove so much emphasis on judgments of "right" and "wrong," in our interactions, and rather see what the overall effect of the maneuver is in terms of its impact on closeness and connectedness. In Taekwondo, for example, an ATTACK is something that we prepare for so that we have the strength, training, and reflexes to escape a dangerous situation without injury. The agility we gain through education, preparation, and practice arms us with the confidence to sidestep danger, and avoid overreacting, and behaving in a way that is more forceful than what the situation warranted. By committing to such a practice, we gain skills to preserve our personal safety while more elegantly navigating our most important relationships.

In the world of boundaries, a *subtle* attack can be even more powerful than an overt one. Balance is crucial in these competitive arts, and it is helpful to recognize that repeated, subtle attacks have the effect of throwing an opponent off balance. Such interactions are the things that bring in trophies in the world of competitive sports, where the object is to demonstrate prowess and superiority. Long-term, intimate relationships, on the other hand, do not bode well in this kind of competitive environment, where winning is about connectedness and deepening of intimacy.

The word VICTIM is also used in the most broad sense imaginable. None of us want to be identified as ABUSERS or VICTIMS, but it's helpful to use these terms in the least pejorative, and most compassionate manner possible. To be an ABUSER is to breach another's boundaries, whether it's done consciously or unconsciously. To be a VICTIM is to be a person whose boundary is being or has been violated. A person can rapidly change from being a victim to being an aggressor, from being infringed upon to violent overreaction, thus becoming an aggressor.

At the risk of complicating things even further, I'm going to be throwing into this mess another complicated creature called "victimstance," which is a posture or stance a person can adopt (consciously or unconsciously) that actually undermines authentic connection in the same ways that other forms of abuse can. This stance constitutes an attempted breach on the boundaries of others; possibly even more powerful and difficult to deal with because of its embedded and covert nature. We will be referring to victimstance as a destructive control behavior. And yes, it is most certainly, a form of abuse.

That having been said, "victimstance" should not be confused with the temporary condition of being on the receiving end of a slimy maneuver, a manipulation, or something another person says that just throws us off balance. In such a case, we might consider for a brief moment, using the term victim to describe our situation. The difference is that the person who uses victimstance as a destructive control behavior identifies, on a more chronic or lasting basis, with a status of victimhood and uses this stance in attempts to get their needs met. Please go to **Appendix** I (on page 38) now for Clinton S. Clark's anecdotal take on victimstance.

Disclaimer

During this course, we will not be discussing physical violence. We will refer to the nonphysical and energetic phenomenon of boundaries with a variety of terms including violence, abuse and manipulation, and destructive control behaviors. We will use classical narcissism and addiction to help us conjure the caricatures that will be useful for identifying the behaviors in their extreme and most destructive forms. None of these terms will be used in a way intended to incriminate or blame anyone in the past or the present. Instead, the terms will help us learn to identify and name specific destructive behaviors, and thereby learn what we can do to reduce or eliminate them from our lives. In studying the extreme examples of boundary violations that we see with addicts and "hard-core" abusers, we can more readily identify subtler forms of abuse when we come across them. At this point, it might be a good idea to point out the difference between blame and accountability. Please see Appendix II (on page 43) for a short reading by Carl Alasko, Ph.D.

Emotional Impoverishment

Many adults are socially and emotionally impoverished. This means that their social and emotional needs were not met as children. When a child grows up in this kind of environment, they learn that the world is generally not a safe place, and that it is not safe or appropriate to have or communicate boundaries. They thus adapt to this impoverished environment in order to survive, internalizing the belief that boundaries are wrong. Part of this adaptation involves cutting one's self off from his or her feelings, because when they expressed emotions, they were punished or humiliated.

When a child is raised in this way, he or she enters adulthood without important skills. If they become parents, they pass these deficits on to their children by parenting them in the same ways they were parented. Parents who are socially and emotionally impoverished have little or no understanding of the importance of a consistent emotional connection to their child during the early years that is so crucial to the development of the healthy self, and the ability to set and maintain healthy boundaries. Please see **Appendix III** (on page 45) for a set of tables created by mental health professionals Barry and Janae Weinhold, that outline the skills that are developmentally appropriate for infants and children at various stages, and the responsibilities of their caregivers to ensure that their children achieve these important landmarks.

Adults who have not mastered the tasks and gained their respective skills are walking around looking quite grown-up, while on the inside, they are very much like children, lacking the skills to ask for or even recognize what they need. The fact that they lack necessary life skills and possess a backlog of unmet emotional needs is embarrassing and often very shameful to them, so they do what they can to hide this deficiency, very often even from themselves (See **Appendix IV** on page 54 for some elucidation on denial). These adults very often end up in parenting roles, their needs still unmet. Parenting provides countless opportunities to bring into consciousness the vulnerable feelings of childhood (see **Appendix V** on page 56 for an article by Trina Brunk about conscious parenting), though not all parents are able to capitalize on this opportunity to grow and mature. The extent to which parents remain unconsciously needy is the extent to which they unknowingly use their children to meet their own needs.

Types of Boundary Violations

According to Clinton S. Clark, "as infants we were unable to set boundaries except in our own way (crying, spitting up, etc). We had not yet learned how to set boundaries in an adult way. As infants, we gave our power to someone else who we thought knew how to take care of us. Of course they did their best, and giving them our power was the only choice we had when we were infants." As adults, we are better positioned to set boundaries, but over and over again, we find ourselves in situations where we feel powerless to set a boundary with another person. Setting boundaries is not something we should expect ourselves to just begin doing overnight.

If boundary setting skills were not modeled or otherwise taught to us, there are things we need to do and learn and other things we need to unlearn before we can become masters. What follows is a list of boundary violations. If the boundary violation on your mind is not included here, please jot it down and bring it to class. It will help me to shape the material of Weeks 2-5 to better meet your needs, and will enrich my collection at the same time!

Invasion of Personal Space Without Permission

Personal space can mean different things in different contexts. In a library or coffee shop, your personal space might be the table you're sitting at, along with all the chairs at that table. It could also mean that energetic bubble around you that extends out to the tips of your fingers if they were outstretched. A bathroom, a bedroom, or a personal belonging such as a cell phone, a personal computer, or a purse or wallet might be an extension of your personal space. According to Clinton S. Clark, any act of invading another person's personal space without permission amounts to boundary violation. Even staring (as a way to invade), or looking through or at someone else's personal effects without permission are forms of invasion of personal space.

Excessive Probing

Excessive probing is also a boundary violation. Excessive probing happens when a person probes for information without regard for the target's willingness or desire to share that information. In doing so, the person fails to honor the other's privacy. When a person with "more power" in the relationship does this, he or she implies that he or she is entitled to this information. In fact, we are in no way obligated to anyone to share the contents of our inner world.

Coercion (the threat of violence, death, and rage)

According to Clinton S. Clark, "The emotional effects of coercion are more damaging to a child than a child who has been beaten. A child growing up in coercion will always be wishing for something (bad) to happen in order for them to relieve their anxiety of waiting for something (bad) to happen."

Rage

Anger is a normal and natural emotion. When anger is used to control or manipulate another person, it is rage. Abuse happens when the person sharing space with the angry or enraged person is a child, is incapable of leaving the vicinity safely, or when the energy of anger is shared without first securing a willing audience from the listener. Anger, like any other emotion, is a personal experience. When it is shared irresponsibly, it is a boundary violation.

Punishing

Not to be confused with natural or reasonable and mutually agreed-upon consequences, punishment is an attempt to control another's behavior by taking away something desired, or otherwise inflicting pain. In its most destructive form, it involves a withdrawal of love (emotional blackmail), and is a maneuver popular among addict parents. Modeled by adults to their children, punishing as a way to control others is carried into the adult lives of many co-dependents. What makes it different from natural consequences is that it is applied unilaterally, often arbitrarily, and without consistency or predictability. Information that might attempt to explain this behavior is withheld as a means to inflict pain and confusion and maintain "power over" the victim. "Silent Treatment" is one example of punishing as a boundary violation.

Blaming

Blaming is a way of assuming a "power over" position in a relationship in order to avoid feelings of vulnerability, and is often done unconsciously. Chronic blaming results in a feeling of walking on eggshells in a relationship. What makes this boundary violation especially toxic is that it is largely only implied – an internal event of the person doing it, and is therefore very hard to address.

Playing the Victim

Also referred to in this Study Guide as victimstance. You may wish to review **Appendix I** (on page 38) here.

Presumptions

It is a violation of my boundaries when you expect me to be a certain way, or to assume a particular role or responsibility. The fact of the matter is, we all experience changes in mood, goals, energy level, and even identity. And certainly, it is our prerogative to change our minds. Moreover, it is a boundary violation for you to tell me what I believe, what my intentions are, or what I think, without first inquiring as to my position on the matter. Again, very little of who I am is static, and is subject to change from one day to the next – even one minute to the next. According to Clinton S. Clark, "If someone needs to know something about me, they may choose to ask me and not presume.... Presumption is a block to communication." The difference between presumption and non-presumption is the difference between an attack and a question. Examples of presumptions follow:

- You're just stubborn/lazy/shy/excited/small /slow/etc. (labels that judge negatively).
- You're living in a dream world.
- I (or You) know you're only doing this to ....
- I know what you're thinking, and it's wrong.
- You're not fooling me. I know exactly what you're up to.
- You're pretty/talented/good/so helpful/nice/quick/ smart/etc. (labels that create expectation).

Judging

A close relative to blaming and presumptions, judging is also a boundary violation, as it automatically places the one doing it in a position of superiority, and the victim in a position of inferiority, creating distance and destroying possibilities for true relating by establishing a "one-up" position.

Shaming

Shaming is the projection of self-non-acceptance onto another person. In the parenting realm, it communicates to a child that he or she is not okay. As adults, we carry the beliefs we acquired from the adults in our childhood lives until we bring them to consciousness, feel the feelings around them, and then formulate and integrate healthier new beliefs. See **Appendix VI** (on page 61) to see common assumptions made by children and carried through adulthood.

Lecturing

According to Clinton S. Clark, "Talking in 'lecture form' is a type of emotional neglect or abandonment. Lecturing a child is talking to a child or at a child without asking them for their opinion or listening to them in return. It's a one sided conversation where the [adult] uses the child in order to expel internal feelings or thoughts. The child's identity or 'emotional self' is not acknowledged or affirmed in a conversation that uses lecture form." Adult caretakers often lecture their children, thinking that they are instilling important values. If the parent does this with no genuine interest in what the child thinks and feels, and no sensitivity as to whether this information is desired, this is a boundary violation.

Talking At

In the adult world, being forced to listen is also a boundary violation. If someone comes to me with an urgent need to expel or vent, and proceeds to talk to me with no consideration for my ability to attend to them and their crisis, and leaves no opening for me to express a need to extract myself, this is a boundary violation.

Compulsive Caretaking/Forced Helping

Co-dependents and addicts for the most part do not wait until they have been asked for help. They force help. According to Clark, "forced help" is a boundary violation. The addict or co-dependent is "operating on the principal that a child is an object of use and therefore does not need to be asked for permission to be used." In adult life, this extends out to partners and spouses that become the addict or co-dependent's next "project," or distraction from their own inner turmoil or pain.

Approval Seeking

Approval seeking is an attempt to control people and situations. Yielding to another's preferences and desires, and making decisions based on those preferences and desires (without taking responsibility for one's own position or preference) can be a boundary violation. For many people who lack skill or confidence in boundary setting, the desire to avoid conflict may be so great that they believe it is safer to "go along to get along" than to show up authentically in relationship.

Excessive Explaining

This boundary violation combines the features of "Talking At" and "Approval Seeking," with the ultimate objective of managing or controlling another's opinion or response to your position.

Chaos

See **Appendix VII** (page 63)

Parentification of Children

This boundary violation is the mother of countless others. Though it is usually not included in lists of boundary violations, it needs to be. According to Terrence Real, "The ultimate boundary violation happens [when children] become caretakers to their own caretakers. When this happens, they often enjoy inordinate power within the family. Nobody can stand up to them." But, as Real points out, "that inordinate power is based on forfeiting the most precious part of them... their souls, their deepest vulnerabilities and needs." In other words, too much responsibility too soon, is a boundary violation which results in the abandonment of the child's primary task: to figure out who they are and what they are here do to for themselves.[1]

Other Boundary Violations (feel free to jot down whatever comes to mind)

Effects of Growing Up Without Boundaries

- Fear of other people's judgment resulting in chronic procrastination.

- Having no limits in response to not feeling good enough.

- Trying to "people please" or seek approval of others.

- Negatively judging other people as a way to distract one's self from intolerable emotions.

---

[1] Real, T. (1997). *I Don't Want to Talk About It: Overcoming the Secret Legacy of Male Depression* (p. 180). Scribner, NY 1997.

- Blaming others for their feelings.

- Feeling uneasy or suspicious when receiving compliments or gifts.

- Assigning more value to completing a task than to the people involved.

- Compulsion to know how something is going to turn out.

- Anxiety about not having control of the things going on in the environment.

- Extreme guilt when standing up for oneself.

Melody Beatty is the author of many excellent books on codependency. Following is a list from her book *Beyond codependency: And getting better all the time.* It describes the unwritten rules a co-dependent family typically follows.[2]

Rules for the Co-Dependent Family

- Don't feel or talk about feelings.

- Don't think, figure things out, or make decisions—you probably don't know what you want or what's best for you.

---

[2] Beattie, M. (1989). *Beyond codependency: And getting better all the time* (pp 93-94). Hazeldon, Center City, MN.

- Don't identify, mention, or solve problems—it's not okay to have them.

- Be good, right, perfect, and strong.

- Don't be who you are because that's not good enough.

- Don't be selfish, put yourself first, say what you want and need, say no, set boundaries, or take care of yourself—always take care of others and never hurt their feelings or make them angry.

- Don't have fun, be silly or enjoy life—it costs money, makes noise and isn't necessary.

- Don't trust yourself, your Higher Power, the process of life or certain people—instead put your faith in untrustworthy people; then act surprised when they let you down.

- Don't be open, honest, and direct—hint, manipulate, get others to talk for you, guess what they want and need and expect them to do the same for you.

- Don't get close to people—it isn't safe.

- Don't disrupt the system by growing or changing.

You can probably see how living in such a family would tend to give a child doubts as to whether he or she can actually survive in the world, without the "care" of the dysfunctional family unit. Such upbringing not only discourages a child from developing healthy distinctions between one's self and others, but also puts a perplexing spin on emotions and self-responsibility. Below is another alternative for you to consider — also from Melody Beattie.[3]

My New Rules

- It's okay to feel my feelings and talk about them when it's safe and appropriate, and I want to.

- I can think, make good decisions, and figure things out.

- I can have, talk about, and solve my problems.

- It's okay for me to be who I am.

- I can make mistakes, be imperfect, sometimes be weak, sometimes be not so good, sometimes be better, and occasionally be great.

- It's okay to be selfish sometimes, put myself first sometimes, and say what I want and need.

- It's okay to give to others, but it's okay to keep some for myself too.

- It's okay for me to take care of me. I can say no and set boundaries.

- It's okay to have fun, be silly sometimes, and enjoy life.

---

[3] Beattie, M. (1989). *Beyond codependency: And getting better all the time* (pp 97-98). Center City, MN: Hazeldon.

- I can make good decisions about who to trust. I can trust myself. I can trust God, even when it looks like I can't.

- I can be appropriately vulnerable.

- I can be direct and honest.

- It's okay for me to be close to some people.

- I can grow and change, even if that means rocking a bunch of boats.

- I can grow at my own pace.

- I can love and be loved. And I can love me, because I'm lovable. And I'm good enough.

Universal Needs

Each of us is responsible for recognizing our own, very personal and changing needs and limits. This idea contradicts what many of us were taught as children, so adjusting to this idea may take some work, commitment, and perseverance. Many of us have brought a backlog of unmet needs with us from our childhood and would much rather maintain the fantasy that someone else (a soulmate, physician, or expert, perhaps) should be a better authority on what we need or want. Sorry folks, this is a common trap, but you are and always will be your own best, most intimate friend. You will never be able to count on any other single person in this world as you can yourself. So stop waiting around for people to figure out what you want, and work on bringing this information into consciousness, putting it into words, accepting that your needs are normal and real, and healthy, and work toward nurturing and accepting yourself just as you are. It is still possible for you to get what you need. Sometimes it helps to draw on past experience, a situation where you invested massive stores of energy into making someone else happy. Use the same kind of sensitivity, observation, and determination to discern your own preferences and needs and then decide that you are worthy of having your needs met. This is not selfish, but responsible. This is nobody's job but your own. If it helps, think of the parable of the empty cup. You cannot quench the thirst of another if you don't have water in your cup.

In many cases, you will need to enlist the help of another person in this process. Negotiating with others in order to get our needs met is a skill, so don't expect to master it all at once. Moreover, you cannot get everything you want from one person. Learning to ask others for what you want and need is a skill, and it involves humility, awareness, and openness to the authentic answer of the person you are asking. You will learn over time that it is often some person's greatest pleasure to give you just what you need. The trick is to be open to receiving what you need (and accepting it with no hidden strings attached) from the person who is equipped to offer it. Very often we stay stuck in a place where we want something specific from a particular person who is not willing or capable of giving it. Identifying and honoring our needs is also an ongoing process because our needs are not static. See **Appendix VIII** (page 66) for a sample list, taken from Clinton S.

Clark, you can use to begin to identify basic needs and limits for yourself. When we finally realize that we are responsible for meeting our own needs, and stop trying to compulsively guess and meet the needs of others, life becomes a lot more simple. Go ahead. Accept this simple but profound truth. You are worthy of having your needs met, and it is not only possible, but probable that you can have your needs met in this lifetime.

Sometimes it happens
that a woman,
upon realizing how splendid she is in every
way,
goes about setting up her life
so that it is just right in every way.

Building Skills

Boundaries become more possible with the development of a few basic skills:

- Strengthening the ability to tolerate unpleasant emotions.

- Building in a pause before responding to the requests of others.

- Asking for clarification.

Strengthening the ability to tolerate unpleasant emotions

We will talk more about emotions, their function, and their anatomy in the next section. For now, know that emotions are a vital part of your internal compass, and that though we might have a habit of avoiding them, they are best accepted and dealt with directly. In fact, when we deal with our emotions directly, they become our friends and allies in knowing when a boundary has been crossed, and what we need to do in response. For some people, the backlog of unaddressed emotions will require the assistance of a qualified professional, so be gentle, go at a pace that is comfortable and safe for you, and don't be afraid to ask for help. Below is a quote from Harriet Braiker, that sets the tone for our work with emotions and boundaries.[4]

> Both fear and anxiety are easily conditioned. This means that after you have been exposed to these negative feelings as a result of the manipulator's effective tactics, you may develop fear and/or anxiety reactions just to being in the presence of the manipulator even when he is not explicitly activating these feelings. Guilt is a uniquely human emotion. It is the result of feeling excessively responsible for the emotions and/or experiences of others. If you are vulnerable or have a well-pulled guilt string, a skilled manipulator can send you on a rocket-

---

[4] Braiker, H. (2004). *Who's pulling your strings? How to break the cycle of manipulation and regain control of your life* (p. 188). New York: McGraw Hill Books.

propelled guilt trip headed for a destination of capitulation and compliance.

When you feel anxiety, fear, or guilt, your response mechanism is propelled into an emergency mode as though a three-alarm fire were raging uncontrolled. The manipulator merely hands you the fire hose and points you in the direction of capitulation and compliance with her desires. The urgency you feel, however, results from the manipulator's pressure and from your overreaction to the discomfort that you feel. It does not come from the reality that a true state of emergency exists. To resist manipulation, you need to alter your reaction to your own negative feelings. The fact is that the anxiety, fear, and guilt manipulators so effectively play on will not cause you to self destruct if you fail to quash them immediately. They certainly will cause you discomfort. But discomfort can be tolerated and withstood. In fact, the longer you allow yourself to stay exposed to the uncomfortable feelings, the more likely it becomes that your discomfort actually will decline in intensity. Psychologists call this phenomenon habituation. However, in order for your fear, anxiety, or guilt to habituate — that is, to decrease in intensity — you must overcome the impulse to jump through the white door [the direction of capitulation and compliance with the manipulator's desires] in order to gain temporary relief.

Just because you are afraid of a manipulator's anger, for example, does not necessarily mean that something dire is really about to happen.

The manipulator likely will get over his anger, and you will tolerate the fear. Or just because you feel guilty for not acquiescing immediately to a manipulative family member's demand, it does not necessarily follow that your relationship with that person will be damaged inalterably or that you will lose their love. Lowering the urgency with which you react to negative feelings and decreasing the intensity of those feelings will have a corrective effect on the emotional reasoning that fuels the manipulative cycle.

Building in a pause before responding to the requests of others

You are sure to meet resistance in your journey to create healthy boundaries for yourself. In the following quote, also from Harriet Braiker,[5] you will have a brief introduction to the second basic skill, that when practiced, will make boundary setting more possible: *THE PAUSE.*

---

[5] Braiker, H. (2004). *Who's pulling your strings? How to break the cycle of manipulation and regain control of your life* (p. 178). New York: McGraw Hill Books.

The first step of resistance is to break that pattern and, in so doing, to recalibrate the power balance of the relationship. You will do this by inserting a period of time between the manipulator's request or demand and your response. Once you learn to build in time to think about your options, your sense of control will increase immediately. When you can make the manipulator live by your timetable instead of his, you take back power. Since you may be in the bad habit of automatically complying or agreeing to your manipulator's requests or demands — agreeing or saying a fast knee-jerk yes before you have given yourself any time to think about them — you will need to break this habit. The best way is to take an immediate breather after the manipulator expresses her request. Telephones lend themselves easily to the insertion of a breather. If you are speaking on the telephone and a manipulator (or a potential manipulator) asks you to do something or go someplace, your immediate response should be something such as:

- I need to put you on hold for a minute or so. Excuse me/thank you.

- I have to ask you to hold the line for a minute. Thanks.

- I need to put the phone down for a minute. Excuse me.

- I'm going to have to call you back in a few minutes. Thank you.

Notice that you are not asking permission. Instead, you are informing the manipulator that you will be taking a minute away from the telephone. This breather allows you to prepare your next statement, which is a play for time. Face-to-face situations require a bit more finesse, but they will still permit you to take a breather in order to break the automatic compliance habit. Excusing yourself from the scene of the interaction for a few minutes is all you will need to interrupt the tendency to immediately say yes or agree to something you would rather avoid. After the request has been made but before you reply, excuse yourself for a few minutes to use the bathroom, make an urgent phone call, get something from your car or office, get some coffee or water, or any other reason you can think of to leave the manipulator alone with her request or demand for a few minutes.

*I have every right to think
before I commit myself
to doing anything for anybody.*

- I need some time to think about what you are saying. I'll get back to you just as soon as I can.

- This issue deserves some real consideration, so I'll need a bit of time to think it over, and I'll let you know as soon as I can.

- I can't give you an answer right now. I will certainly think it over, and I'll get back to you as soon as possible.

- I'm not in a position right now to answer that, but I will get back to you when I am.

- This is an important issue, and I will need some time to give it the thought it deserves. Then, of course, I'll get back to you.

Asking for clarification

Another simple but vital skill is asking for clarification. The following excerpt is from Clinton S. Clark.[6]

The only way for me to understand what someone else's word concepts mean, is to ask them. When the information I'm listening to requires my understanding of the other person's point of view, I ask for clarification. I don't need to get caught up in creating chaos for myself by not asking for clarification.

The key to detaching from the need to rescue is to wait until I've been asked for help. However, I need to keep in mind that people ask in awkward and unclear ways for help. People do the best that they can at the moment and people do what they think they need to do to take care of themselves. Unfortunately, their behavior may also result in miscommunication (or the lack of it).

---

[6] Clark, C. C. (2011). *The art of healing.* Retrieved May 10, 2011, from http://www.healthyplace.com/addictions/art-of-healing/adult-children-of-dysfunctional-families-alcoholism/menu-id-1074/

I can choose to ask for clarification if I think someone is trying to solicit my help, but hasn't actually said:

- "I need your help."

- "Will you help me?"

- "May I have your help for a minute?"

Anatomy of an Emotion

Few people understand that emotions have an important function in our lives and that if they are used correctly, they can actually pave the way for healthier relationships. Emotions, when we learn how to listen to them, let us know when a boundary needs to be established to ensure safety or otherwise meet an important need.

One of the most basic things about emotions that nobody bothered to tell us before was that they actually have a beginning, a middle, and an end. I was in my forties when I first heard it said that when an emotion is experienced without resistance or judgment, it will complete itself and disappear forever within forty seconds. People tend to spend an awful lot of life energy suppressing emotions while the fact of the matter is, a tremendous amount of relief and healing can happen through the experiencing of the emotions we've avoided for so long. Interestingly, there is a very good reason people avoid feeling their feelings. Either we have been taught at a very young age that it's not okay to feel emotions, or it simply wasn't safe to express our emotions, and if we did, we would risk humiliation, manipulation, or punishment of some sort. Still others experienced intense emotions as children and nobody was available to help them understand what was happening. In such cases, the child learned to disconnect from the intense feeling because it was intolerable and would have been too overwhelming to experience. The energy of such an emotion does not simply go away, but is walled off in the individual in much the same way as a cyst in the body is, to be dealt with at a later time.

Emotions have an inside and an outside part. The inside part is the signal we experience on the inside, whether it's an uneasy feeling, a clinching, a clutching, a flutter, heat, or the change in a vital body function. This signal is part of an ingenious system to preserve life, and is designed to propel us to attend to an important need. Since so many of us have been trained to ignore our emotions, reconnecting with them may be uncomfortable at first. Therefore, it may be necessary for you to navigate intense or overwhelming emotions with the help of a qualified professional or with the permission of a capable and safe friend.

The outside part of an emotion is the collection of cues visible to the outside world. A reddening of the face, a tensing of the muscles, tightening of the jaw, tears, sobs, a flinch: these are all involuntary physical events that are visible to the outside world. Unlike the various voluntary exhibitions of emotion used in attempts to control or manipulate others (pouting, temper tantrums), the outside part of an emotion is an automatic, uncalculated thing. Read more about the anatomy of emotion by Pat Ogden in her book *Trauma and the Body* in **Appendix IX** (page 69).

Emotions tend to begin calling for your attention at the threshold of your ability to safely address them. Emotions might start knocking on the door of your awareness through your dreams, through witnessing others handle them well (or poorly), through television shows, movies, literature, music, education, creative processes. Cultivating awareness is the first step to healing and releasing the energy of old, stored emotions.

Conflict

The setting of boundaries may not be met with approval all around. Conflict gets a bad rap in most cultures, particularly ours, where it is synonymous with fighting. Children are punished when they don't agree. Sadly, many parents are not equipped to model or teach conflict resolution skills, and so these children are faced with two unfortunate choices: to be "good" and avoid conflict, or be labeled "troublemakers" if they continue to speak their truth.

Spouses who are comfortable with the status quo have any number of tactics that squelch or dissuade their partners from bringing up any topic that suggests that something about the relationship needs to change. But don't kid yourself into believing that you can have a sustainable relationship without conflict. As you enter into this project of developing and learning about boundaries, prepare yourself for amazing changes in your life. And yes, it will probably get worse before it gets better.

Henry Cloud, PhD and John Townsend, PhD have contributed volumes to the field of boundaries. Check out **Appendix X** (page 74) for their take on conflict.

Guilt

Many of us have been raised in families that implied that our boundaries were bad or inappropriate, or at the very least inconvenient to the people around us. Many of us learned by watching others or picking up on the cues of others that it was our responsibility to keep others happy, or to step in and do for others what was theirs to do for themselves. These were the roles we adopted in the culture that was our family, and being in these roles was the only way we knew. If we broke these unwritten, mostly unspoken rules, we faced a nagging feeling that we were wrong or bad. Now that we are on the road to recovery, authentic relating, and enduring intimacy, we have to develop a new relationship with guilt. We begin to notice guilt and respond to it just like we would any other emotion. We experience the physical sensation of it, we examine the thoughts that come along with the feeling, and we resist the urge to respond impulsively. We give ourselves permission to make a conscious decision about how we will respond. We can write down the thoughts that come to us in a moment of excruciating guilt in order to examine their appropriateness, their value. We can take a step back and assess their validity, their usefulness. We can decide if they are worthy of the space they are occupying in our brains. Most of these thoughts are in desperate need of an upgrade.

Now is the perfect time to replace the old, destructive thoughts with more affirming, accurate, and self honoring thoughts. Often, the simple act of recognizing the old programming is enough to move you through the guilt safely, without allowing it to propel you into behaving in old, unhealthy ways based on fear, self-sacrifice, and self-denial. See **Appendix XI** (page 77) for some excerpts from Cloud & Townsend's book *Boundaries: When to Say Yes, How to Say No To Take Control of Your Life.*

Forgiveness

Refusing to forgive has been compared to eating rat poison with the expectation that it will take care of the rat. This comparison offers an amusing image that illustrates beautifully how important forgiveness is in the maintenance of healthy boundaries. While forgiveness is touted as admirable, beware of the impulse to forgive before you have honestly faced the truth about what has happened, and processed any strong emotions that come up around this information. If you find that you are having trouble forgiving, it could indicate that you are still in pain, and need to heal before you are ready to think about forgiveness.

Forgiving ourselves for past mistakes is also an important step toward mending our self esteem, and will ultimately help us feel worthy of the safety and protection that boundaries offer. Cloud and Townsend have a straightforward perspective on the topic of forgiveness from a Christian perspective in their book, *Boundaries: When to Say Yes, How to Say No to Take Control of Your Life.* See an excerpt in **Appendix XII** (page 79).

Suggested Reading

Alasko, C. (2008) Emotional bullshit: The hidden plague that is threatening to destroy your relationships—and how to stop it. New York: Penguin Group.

Brunk, T. (2011) Conscious parenting: Uncovering perfectionism's game, [nterrupting trauma & abuse cycles. Retrieved Feb. 6, 2012 from http://www.trina brunk.com/music3/2010/11/18/being-still-like-a-log-conscious-parenting-vs-perfect-parenting/

Beattie, M. (1989). Beyond codependency: And getting better all the time. Center City, MN: Hazeldon.

Behary, W. T. (2003). *Disarming the narcissist: Surviving and thriving with the self-absorbed.* Oakland CA: New Harbinger Publications, Inc.

Braiker, H. (2004). Who's pulling your strings? How to break the cycle of manipulation and regain control of your life. New York: McGraw Hill Books.

Clark, C. C. (2011). *The art of healing.* Retrieved May 10, 2011, from http://www.healthyplace.com/addictions/art-of-healing/adult-children-of-dysfunctional-families-alcoholism/menu-id-1074/

Cloud, H. & Townsend, J. (1992). *Boundaries: When to say yes, how to say no to take control of your life.* Grand Rapids, MI: Zondervan.

Cloud, H & Townsend, J. (2003). *Boundaries face to face: How to have that difficult conversation you've been avoiding.* Grand Rapids, MI: Zondervan.

Evans, P. (2002). *Controlling people: How to recognize, understand, and deal with people who try to control you.* Avon, MO: Adams Media Corporation.

Masters R. A. (2008). *Compassionate wrath: Transpersonal approaches to anger.* Retrieved Nov. 6, 2008, from http//pods.gaia.com/Robert_augustus_masters/discussions/view/333694?printable=1

McLaren, K. (2010). *The Language of emotions: What your feelings are trying to tell you.* Boulder, CO: Sounds True.

Ogden, P, Minton, K. M., & Pain, C. (2006) *Trauma and the body: A sensorimotor approach to psychotherapy.* New York: W.W. Norton & Company, Inc.

Pierrakos, E. (1990) *The pathwork of self-transformation.* New York: Bantam Books.

Real, T. (1997) *I don't want to talk about it: Overcoming the secret legacy of male depression.* New York: Scribner.

Siegel, Daniel J. & Hartzell, M. (2004). *Parenting from the inside out.* New York: Penguin Group (USA) Inc.

Weinhold, J. & Weinhold, B. (2008). *The flight from intimacy:*

Healing your relationship of counter-dependency – the other side of co-dependency. Novato, CA: New World Library.

Wolf, A. E. (1991) *Get out of my life but first could you drive me and Cheryl to the mall?* HarperCollinsCanandaLtd.

Weinhold, B. K. & Weinhold, J. B. (2008). *Breaking free of the co-dependency.* Novato, CA: New World Library.

Appendices

Appendix I Playing The Victim...38

Appendix II Blame Versus Accountability.............................43

Appendix III Developmental Tasks and Skills....................... 45

Appendix IV The Toxic Trio... 54

Appendix V Conscious Parenting.. 56

Appendix VI Negative Assumptions from Childhood.......... 61

Appendix VII Chaos...63

Appendix VIII Basic Needs and Limits................................... 66

Appendix IX Emotions..69

Appendix X Conflict..74

Appendix XI Guilt...77

Appendix XII Forgiveness..79

Appendix XIII Working Definitions..81

Appendices are made up entirely of excerpts from other authors. Please indulge your interest and learn more by reading your personal favorites. A bibliography/reading list is included on page 33.

Appendix I

Playing the Victim

Playing the Victim is an extremely effective technique used to control someone (especially children). The addict parent controls the child's behavior by becoming the so-called wounded victim. The child might say or do something that the addict parent becomes uncomfortable with. In reaction to the child's behavior, the addict parent responds by saying something like this:

(said from an angry victimstance)

"How could you do that to your mother?"
"Mommy thinks you don't love her anymore."
"You don't care about me at all, do you?"
"You're hurting mommy. You're driving her crazy and no one will be able to take care of you then!"

This destructive control behavior uses false guilt to control the child. When the addict parent plays the victim, the child looks inward and thinks: "How could I do that to my parent...She (or He) looks so hurt and sounds so angry or depressed...She's (or He's) talking and looking at me; therefore I must have caused her (or his) pain...I'd better be good so I don't hurt her (or him) any more...she's (or he's) the only one I have to take care of me and the alternative of taking care of myself scares me to death, because that's impossible for myself as a child to do. I could die. I'm sure I'd die.

The goal of an addict who is addicted to their child is to "feel better" by controlling the child. [For the addict], control is equated to compliance and compliance is equated to no frustration. No frustration or conflict is equated to security and security equates to happy addict. Unfortunately, children of addict parents grow up full of false guilt or shame as a result of being trained by the addict parent's use of playing the victim. They (the children) automatically feel guilty, terrified, and anxious when they come in contact with anyone playing the victim.

Children who are trained to be objects of an addiction receive the following message from their addict parents:

I'm not OK, when .... You're not

Toni's Translation: I have no coping skills for feeling bad or tolerating strong emotions (mine or yours). If I'm around you when you are having needs, setting boundaries or otherwise being yourself, I believe you to be the source of my pain. I can't allow you to be yourself if I feel bad in the process.

Unfortunately, a child does not have the benefit of insight into this translation. He or she only knows that their addict parent is not ok when they (the child) are not ok. The child then rationalizes that:

If the addict parent is not ok, who is going to take care of me?

In response to this rationale, they believe that by being ok enough, their addict parent (their provider) will be ok enough to take care of them. The alternative as seen by the child is death (Whitfield, 1988). They think, "If I don't take care of my addict parent by being ok, they are not going to be able to take care of me (because they won't be ok enough to do so). And, if they aren't ok enough to take care of me, I could die. I am not old enough or knowledgeable enough to take care of myself."

This is the terror.
This is the helplessness.
This is the anger, rage, and pain.

Codependents blame other people for how they feel. Obviously, if a codependent is attached to you, they are going to blame you for how they feel. They've been trained to believe that their feelings are the results of other people's actions and feelings.

Children of addict parents learn that in order to stay accepted in their family they must remain easy to use, and be without boundary (do nothing to frustrate the addict). Children of addict parents learn how to become easy to use by becoming invisible; which means to become compliant and without needs, or suffer the consequences of being apparent, real, noticeable, with boundaries, and having needs.

This phenomena is also described by Whitfield (1989) and Cermak (1986) as "psychic numbing." Children raised as objects of addiction are under attack or the threat of attack throughout the duration of their childhood and sometimes beyond. They are like combat soldiers waiting for an attack to occur. Cermak (1986) writes that during periods of extreme stress, such as an attack or the waiting for an attack to occur (the threat of death, injury, and the feeling of being unable to flee), "combat soldiers are often called upon to act regardless of how they are feeling. Their survival depends upon their ability to suspend feelings in favor or taking steps to ensure their safety." This is a characteristic of Post-Traumatic Stress Disorder or PTSD. In the case of children trained to be objects of addiction, you might say that they were forced into fighting a war without weapons to protect themselves and they were unable to see the enemy. This is one of the reasons why so many children of dysfunctional families withdraw into isolation. It's the last resort in fighting an unseen enemy and fighting an enemy without a weapon of defense. You might say that this [material] is an exposure of the enemy by exposing the attack methods, i.e., the destructive control behaviors that hurt.

As objects of addiction, **these children have psychologically trained their feelings to become unavailable to them as a way to cope with repeated attacks or the threat of attack**. As a result of this, their feelings have become so unavailable to them that they subsequently become emotionally and cognitively unaware of an attack at the time it occurs.

[In the case of me, in my addictive patterns, here is how it works for my daughter.] Over time, it will become painfully apparent to her that her actions and feelings will somehow trigger me. She will become a "people pleaser" to avoid having to deal with my reactions to her. She knows she can't be herself without me reacting to her, so she becomes what she thinks I want her to be. This is how children of [addicts and] codependents learn to survive. They can't be themselves so they become what they think will keep them from getting hurt.

She'll learn how to control other people by being a "people pleaser." She'll become very good at guessing how I feel and very poor at knowing how she feels. Her focus will become directed towards other people outside of herself. She'll obsessively try to figure out what everyone else needs and not be able to figure out what she needs. And if someone resents her for trying to take care of their needs without being asked, she will become angry and resentful because it scares her not to take care of someone else.

References

Cermak, T. L. (1986). Diagnosing & Treating Co-Dependence: A Guide for Professionals who Work with Chemical Dependents, Their Spouses, and Children. Minneapolis, MN: Johnson Institute.

Whitfield, C. L. (1988). Healing The Child Within. Audio Cassette. Health Communications, Inc. Taped live U.S. Journal Training Conference. Chicago. June 1988.

Whitfield, C. L. (1989). Healing The Child Within. Health Communications, Inc.

If you would like to resume reading this material in the order it was intended, please return now to Study Guide, page 6, **Disclaimer**.

Clark, C. C. (2011). The art of healing. Retrieved May 10, 2011, from http://www.healthyplace.com/addictions/art-of-healing/adult-children-of-dysfunctional-families-alcoholism/menu-id-1074/

Appendix II

Blame Versus Accountability

There's a big difference between blame and accountability. It's essential to understand that the two words perform vastly different jobs. Unfortunately, people typically confuse these two terms — to their own detriment. For instance, when I'm discussing a patient's family history that included a great deal of neglect and abuse, the patient will often say, "I don't want to blame my parents for my problems. I love my mom and dad." I try to explain, "Yes, I understand you love your parents, and it's possible to love your parents and also hold them accountable for their neglect and abuse. It's their behaviors that need to be discussed, not their value as people. Holding a person accountable means to separate the behavior from the person's value. There's no need to condemn your parents, or to devalue them as human beings." I often have to go over this idea several times. Why? Because we're used to having the two processes fused into one, even though the dictionary definitions are very different. Blame is defined as: 1. To hold responsible; to accuse. 2. To find fault with; to censure; to condemn. Blame, therefore, is seen as starkly negative. The definition of accountable is far simpler than that: 1. Answerable. 2. Capable of being explained. That's it! There's no suggestion of condemnation or censure.

In other words:

Accountability says:
This is what you did. Period. Stop.

Blame says:
You made this mistake because
there's something wrong with you.

If you would like to resume reading this material in the order it was intended, please return now to Study Guide, page 6 Emotional Impoverishment

Alasko, C. (2008) *Emotional bullshit: The hidden plague that is threatening to destroy your relationships – and how to stop it* (pg 25). New York: Penguin Group.

Appendix III

THE DEVELOPMENTAL STAGES AND ESSENTIAL
DEVELOPMENTAL PROCESSES OF INDIVIDUAL EVOLUTION

Stage of Development and Primary Task
Co-Dependency (Conception to Six Months) **Bonding and
Attachment**
- *Essential Developmental Processes of Individual Evolution*
  - **Mother:**
    - Mother receives good prenatal care and support
  - **Child:**
    - experiences a non-violent birth with immediate
      interventions to heal any birth trauma
    - achieves consistent, secure bonding and
      attachment with mother and/or other adult care-
      givers
    - learns primal trust in parents through a
      consistent resonant connection
    - learns emotional resiliency skills
    - creates a secure internal working model of
      self/other
    - learns healthy emotional communication and
      social engagement skills with parents and
      others
    - bonds securely with siblings and extended
      family
- *Suggested Experiences for Completing The Essential Developmental
  Processes of Individual Evolution*
  - **Mother:**
    - maintains a high-quality diet and reduces
      environmental stressors to prevent the risk of
      cortisol production during pregnancy
    - receives effective postnatal emotional and
      physical support

- provides nurturing, respectful touch and eye contact; she gazes at, sings to, and speaks to the child in loving ways
  - **Parents:**
    - plan for and want the child
    - build prenatal relationship with the child
    - use nonviolent birthing practices
    - nurse and room-in at the hospital and have prolonged skin-to-skin contact between child and each parent in the first 12-24 hours following birth
  - **Child:**
    - gets timely emotional and tactile comforting to help heal developmental traumas caused by disruptions in resonant connection to parents
    - receives unconditional love from parents
    - receives authentic mirroring and validation of his or her essence from parents
  - **Immediate and extended family members:**
    - provide consistent, nurturing, and empathic contact
    - provide comfortable and protective environment to meet the child's needs for safety and survival

Stage of Development and Primary Task
Counter-Dependency (Six to Thirty-six Months) **Separation and Individuation**

- *Essential Developmental Processes of Individual Evolution*
  - **Child:**
    - completes the psychological separation process with parents
    - learns to safely explore his or her environment
    - learns to trust and regulate his or her own thoughts, feelings, and behaviors in socially appropriate ways

- internalizes appropriate physical and social limits
- develops healthy narcissism
- resolves internal conflicts between oneness and separateness (I'm okay, you're okay)
- bonds with self
- continues to build secure internal working model
- completes his or her individuation or psychological birth process

- *Suggested Experiences for Completing The Essential Developmental Processes of Individual Evolution*
  - **Parents:**
    - offer timely help in healing any narcissistic wounds or developmental traumas that interfere with resonance
    - give the child permission and support to safely explore his or her environment; they give the child twice as many yeses as nos during this time
    - rearrange environment to provide safety
    - understand and respect the child's need to develop internal regulation of emotions, especially shame
    - help the child identify self-needs, as opposed to the needs of others
    - model how to directly ask to have one's needs met
    - use nonshaming responses in limit-setting and discipline
    - give positive support for the child's efforts to develop an autonomous Self
  - **Adult Caregivers:**
    - help the child quickly reestablish the resonant connection with the mother when it's disrupted

- offer empathy and compassion as the child learns to regulate his or her conflicting emotions, thoughts, and behaviors
- offer authentic mirroring and validation of the child's essence
- offer permission for the child to be a separate individual and to trust his or her internal impulses

Stage of Development and Primary Task

Independence (Three to Six Years) **Mastery of Self And Environment**

- *Essential Developmental Processes of Individual Evolution*
  - **Child:**
    - learns to cooperate with others
    - learns to negotiate with others to get his or her needs met
    - learns to accept responsibility for his or her personal behaviors and life experiences
    - experiences secure bonding with peers and other adults
    - develops a social conscience
    - bonds securely with his or her culture
    - bonds securely with the planet
    - lives his or her life as an authentic adult
    - bonds securely with own children
    - understands the influence of incomplete developmental processes on his or her life and how to successfully heal developmental traumas
- *Suggested Experiences for Completing The Essential Developmental Processes of Individual Evolution*
  - **Parents:**
    - rearrange home environment to support the child's mastery of self-care (eating, dressing, and toilet training)

- support the child's development of effective internal limits and consequences
- help the child learn appropriate emotional self-regulation and control
- help the child learn to trust his or her inner sense of wisdom and guidance
- provide the child with experiences for the safe exploration of nature
- help the child develop sensory relationships with nature
- provide for reciprocal social interactions with other children
- teach cross-relational thinking, including empathy and respect for others
- help the child develop cause/effect problem-solving skills
- **Immediate and extended family members:** offer nurturing, supportive, and consistent contact
- **Adults** model partnership solutions to conflicts

Stage of Development and Primary Task
Interdependence (Six to Twenty-nine Years) **Cooperation and Negotiation Skills**
- *Essential Developmental Processes of Individual Evolution*
  - **Child:**
    - learns to cooperate with others
    - learns to negotiate with others to get his or her needs met
    - learns to accept responsibility for his or her personal behaviors and life experiences
    - experiences secure bonding with peers and other adults
    - develops a social conscience

- o bonds securely with his or her culture
- o bonds securely with the planet
- o lives his or her life as an authentic adult
- o bonds securely with own children
- o understands the influence of incomplete developmental processes on his or her life and how to successfully heal developmental traumas
- *Suggested Experiences for Completing The Essential Developmental Processes of Individual Evolution*
  - **Parents:**
    - o **Parents** model effective cooperative social engagement skills in couple, family, and peer relationships
  - **Child:**
    - o seeks to learn negotiation skills to get his or her needs met in healthy ways
    - o seeks solutions to his or her conflicts that honor the needs of all parties involved
    - o seeks adult validation of the importance of keeping his or her relationship agreements
    - o seeks an adult model that can teach him or her empathy and compassion for others
    - o seeks adults who can teach him or her intuitive language and thinking skills
    - o seeks nurturing, supportive, and consistent contact from immediate and extended family members
    - o seeks support from parents and other adults on how to build sustainable relationships with other adults and how to find a primary love partner
    - o seeks adult input on the values of his or her cultural group and how to overcome any limits imposed by family and culture

- o seeks personal meaning and a personal mission within the context of the "global family"
- o seeks information and skills for healing his or her developmental traumas
- o seeks assistance in developing systemic and transsystemic thinking

- o **Adults** encourage the development of an internalized "safety parent" allowing safe risk-taking behaviors

If you would like to resume reading this material in the order it was intended, please return now to Study Guide, page 6 Emotional Impoverishment

Weinhold, J. & Weinhold, B. (2008). *The flight from intimacy: Healing your relationship of counter-dependency – the other side of co-dependency* (pp 32-35). Novato, CA: New World Library.

Appendix IV
The Toxic Trio

The Toxic Trio always work together. This fact is crucial to understanding these components. No element is isolated from the other. Whenever a person uses denial, immediately after comes delusion, the creation of a false or distorted reality. And when things fall apart or a person's held accountable, blame is used to shift responsibility. It's a circular, self-supporting process that bears repeating:

1) First an essential fact is denied, then
2) Delusion creates an alternate reality, then
3) Blame shifts the responsibility for the problem.[7]

Denial is so difficult to deal with because it's a fundamental psychological process. It's one of the twenty or so "ego defense mechanisms" that during childhood protect and defend the developing personality, the ego, from too much stress, from the harshness of too much reality. The specific purpose of denial is to allow us to continue living by denying facts that might immobilize us with fear. Or paralyze our efforts to fulfill our needs and desires, even as adults.[8]

Allowing delusion to focus your attention on short-term gain blocks the fulfillment of long-term Core Needs. The result can be serious consequences to your overall emotional and

---

[7] Pg 8

[8] Pg 10

physical health. Once immersed in a delusional reality, you lose your ability to separate fact from fiction. We create a fantasy reality to avoid the discomfort, pain and limits of our actual life because truth can be dull. Truth can hold us down, just like gravity, and limits our ability to act. Creating a delusional version of truth allows us to operate beyond ordinary, tedious restrictions.[9]

Delusion can expand a detail into the whole picture. When you're in the grip of delusion, it's all too easy to take a small part of the picture and expand it to create a totally different reality, a version of the truth that allows you to get what you want when you want it.[10]

If you would like to resume reading this material in the order it was intended, please return now to Study Guide, page 6 Emotional Impoverishment

Alasko, C. (2008) *Emotional bullshit: The hidden plague that is threatening to destroy your relationships – and how to stop it.* New York: Penguin Group.

---

[9] Pg 21

[10] Pg 23

Appendix V

Conscious Parenting: Uncovering Perfectionism's Game, Interrupting Trauma & Abuse Cycles

Clearly, it can be challenging to stay conscious as a parent. I think that as a spiritual practice, it has to be a fast-track to enlightenment. It's just that so many of us haven't engaged it that way because to do so requires immense courage and faith, and there aren't many examples available to us. It is much easier on Sunday to put the kids in daycare and get our enlightenment in the sanctuary with all the other polite adults. We can ignore our traumatized places and put on our happy perfect faces.

I've been interested in conscious parenting since I was a little girl. I remember listening to my mom yell at me about cleaning my room and thinking she could get a lot further with me if she would just talk respectfully. I promised myself that if I ever had kids, I would do a better job than she. While my mom was all about being in control at all times, I was full of dreams about creating mutual wins, treating each other respectfully, and having fun together.

And now that I'm a mom, (you knew this was coming) I can understand and appreciate my mom a lot more. Although our styles are different, I know now that it would be arrogant to even imply that I could do a better job than she did. I have found being a parent can be all at once humbling, mystifying, thrilling and sometimes shattering. Not such good news to my ego.

Perfect Parenting vs. Conscious Parenting

Conscious Parenting isn't about being perfect, another opportunity for you to feel guilty and nail yourself for getting it all wrong. It's the opposite of perfectionism, which, while it seems harmless, is key in keeping the painful story going.

Perfect is focused on behavior and appearances.

Conscious is focused on the inner experience.

Perfect is about forcing or controlling to bring about a desired outcome in the future.

As a conscious parent, my priority is connection and bringing my awareness to the present moment.

Perfectionism seeks approval in vain. Funny, I almost wrote "vein", which expresses it maybe better — seeking an intravenous infusion of approval from an outside source, a drug that must constantly be sought but that never, ever gives the deep nourishment we really need . . . its futile quest is to medicate an imagined deficit. And that's the trap, because you'll never be good enough when you're judged against an illusion. That's what perfection does: sets up an illusory, unattainable goal, and then accepts nothing less. Do we really want to hold ourselves and our children up to this unforgiving measure? Failure is guaranteed; the soul has no choice but to express through dysfunction.

Consciousness experiences being in the moment. There is no lack, no right & wrong way to behave: instead, a deeper awareness of the love that we are guides our decisions. We get to live deeper lives when we engage life consciously. Yes, it can be messy — but so worth it.

Consciousness naturally releases us from the hold of past trauma, while perfectionism ensures that trauma is perpetuated.

Using triggers to track down and transform cycles of trauma and abuse

It's cliche' to talk about parenting as being the most difficult job in the world. I think it's a mistake to blame that on children. I think it's challenging to engage parenting consciously specifically because of all the trauma we carry from generations and lives past. Unless we can find ways that work for us to heal and release the cycles of trauma and abuse, we'll pass them on.

Toni A. Rahman, LCSW is a counselor and therapist in Columbia, Missouri. She sees clients every day who are grappling with the various manifestations of trauma, and she supports individuals and families in releasing painful patterns and claiming renewed lives. According to Toni, "Trauma comes in all shapes and sizes and tends to plague us all to varying degrees at one time or another, whether it's the Big-T Trauma of an automobile accident or the loss of a loved one, or the smaller-t trauma a child experiences when encountering emotions that he or she can't yet put into words."

When we live with the effects of unhealed trauma, it can be hard to think clearly and respond appropriately to what is really present — we're caught in a loop trying to address something that happened in the past. When we're with young children who have not yet learned to dodge the places where we're traumatized, we can feel our painful places triggered constantly. Which is exhausting!

In my journey in moving from perfectionism to conscious

parenting, I have found these triggers to be a powerful opportunity for healing and growth. Even while it may feel awful at the time, a trigger always points directly to something that I've hidden from myself due to past trauma, but that will hinder my growth and healing until it is revealed and released.

My personal practice has been that when I feel deeply triggered, to "be like a log" — do nothing, just observe myself, and pay attention to my breath.

One big trigger for me is when my two young sons fight. I can't tell you how many times I've told them to stop fighting with each other. I've told them to make up and be friends and the battle intensifies. I've screamed at them and threatened them and been big scary monster mommy. No luck. "Being Like A Log" can sometimes be excruciating because it calls to my present awareness some old long-forgotten pain that had been too much for me to handle at the time and which I had stashed away for such a moment as this.

What I first notice are the beliefs flying around in my head about the situation. "He's evil." "He must be punished." "I have to put a stop to this." The next thing that comes to my awareness is the intensity of my feelings — often grief, rage, terror. Always, the feelings I have are out of context with what is actually happening between the boys in the present moment. They are feelings left over from what happened in the past. Any actions I take while in this state will be similarly out of context, and I'm at risk of being abusive myself.

I sit and be still, and watch my breath, and feel my feelings. I also find prayer to be very powerful. I ask for help in healing and releasing the trauma, as necessary — sometimes, the trigger is so great and my mind is mush, and asking for help is all I can think of to do. But it's enough. And I feel myself coming more into the present moment.

Often after giving myself some space, watching my breath, connecting with myself and feeling my feelings, almost like magic, I notice that the children are playing delightedly with each other. Doing and saying things together that are so beautiful to me that they bring tears to my eyes.

Now, please be clear — I am NOT saying that I think it's a bad idea when kids are fighting with each other or bullying to set firm limits and re-direct and give information about how to get needs met in a positive way. I most certainly do think that these are important skills. What I'm talking about is recurring situations where you're feeling really triggered, where you feel the pressure rising and it feels all too familiar — you are concerned that you might flip out and act in a way that damages your relationship with your child.

Take the test

Do you see yourself as being someone who's relatively free from trauma? A great test is this — play with your child. Let them take the lead. Do what they choose. Do it for 15 minutes — set a timer and don't look at your watch for the duration. Notice how you feel. Do you feel refreshed and invigorated and in love with the young person you're with? Or are you feeling drained, frustrated, bored, antsy? Can't wait for it to be over? Sometimes I struggle with staying awake while playing with my four-year-old, but have a very easy time hanging out with my seven-year-old, which tells me that there's material ripe for healing my inner four-year-old, and that I'm pretty clear at the inner seven-year-old level.

If you find yourself experiencing some stuck places, do yourself and your family a favor and get help! You didn't deserve what happened to you, and you and your family deserve to be free of painful patterns. Don't isolate. Whether through reaching out to a friend, committing to a course of therapy, spending time in nature, praying and asking for prayers of others, there is help available. Yes, it takes courage! But when we engage the process of becoming more conscious, we can begin to release the wounds of countless generations, and set into motion a new way of being that will bless countless generations to come.

If you would like to resume reading this material in the order it was intended, please return now to Study Guide, page 8 Types of Boundary Violations

Brunk, T. (2011) Conscious parenting: Uncovering perfectionism's game, [interrupting trauma & abuse cycles. Retrieved Feb. 6, 2012 from http://www.trina brunk.com/music3/2010/11/18/being-still-like-a-log-conscious-parenting-vs-perfect-parenting/

Appendix VI

Negative Assumptions Originating from Childhood

Internalized during a moment of vulnerability, when a child hasn't sufficient support to process or feel the emotions around a difficult experience, the following (usually mostly unconscious) negative assumptions are common ways shame dwells in the body. Because of their unconscious nature, and the resistance to feeling the emotions they carry, such assumptions continue to subtly influence choices and behavior.

- I'm unworthy
- I'm stupid
- I'm bad
- I'm insignificant
- I'm not okay the way I am
- I'm permanently damaged
- I'm ridiculous
- I'm an idiot
- I can't do anything right
- There's something wrong with me

Adding blame to shame, a child learns to grow up feeling as though he or she is the source of others' problems. Here are the negative internal beliefs that arise from this type of childhood event.

- It's my fault
- I'm not to be trusted

- I'm selfish
- I'm lazy

Not having basic needs or worthiness affirmed denies a child a sense of safety in the world. Such an environment imprints a child with the following negative cognitions:

- It's not okay to be me
- It's not safe to have emotions
- It's not okay to express emotions
- My feelings are a problem to others
- I'm overly sensitive
- I'm a wimp
- I can't trust my senses
- I won't be loved if I express dissent
- My needs are too much
- My needs are not important
- I'm a burden

If you would like to resume reading this material in the order it was intended, please return now to Study Guide, page 12 Lecturing

Appendix VII

Chaos

Chaos defined as: An inner turmoil process that allows me to maintain a level of terror that exceeds or matches the terror I experienced in childhood. A state of internal unrest.

> Chaos keeps me from having
> an intimate relationship with myself.
> An intimate relationship with myself is:
> Knowing how I feel, Knowing what I like,
> Knowing what I don't like, and
> Knowing what I think.

Not having learned the skills of how to cope with how I feel in a safe and nurturing way has made it a terrifying process for me to acknowledge strong feelings. It's like parachuting from a plane without knowing how to operate the parachute. Addicts lack the coping skills for having strong feelings. The terror of being helpless (unable to cope with), is suppressed or distracted from consciousness by engaging in chaos. Addicts are said to be addicted to excitement. The excitement is chaos. Engaging in chaos is a way to separate myself from my feelings. This is the first function of chaos.

The second function of chaos is to generate enough chaos to maintain a terror level that equals or exceeds the terror experienced in childhood. The levels of chaos and terror have become so high, that the lack of it feels unnerving or scary. It's like being abandoned. "I almost wish something terrible would happen in order to relieve the anxiety of waiting for something to happen." As a result of being normalized to chaos and terror in childhood, I continue to create chaos and terror as a way to experience feeling secure (recreate my childhood norm) in my life now. It maintains a constant state of preparedness.

Most of my chaos is created as a response to feeling scared to death or unworthy. I am worthy and it hurts to feel unworthy in the company of another person or a thing that treats me in an unworthy way. I may be blinding myself to an intense hurt with the "chaos" I create in a situation as a way to avoid acknowledging the hurt. No matter how healthy I am it hurts to be treated as unworthy by someone I would like to treat me as being worthy.

The opposite of this double bind is asking for my needs to be met and going elsewhere when they become unavailable to me without the destruction of myself (my spirit, awareness, or consciousness) or someone else in the process. What I call the freedom for you and I to explore the lives we've chosen and express ourselves without feeling the need to use destructive control behaviors; and without feeling terrorized.

Carrying guilt and shame as a way to create chaos. Avoiding making amends.

Lacking a healthy knowledge of my limits in order to create chaos by having expectations too high to meet. Over doing everything. Refusing the right to have limits. Saying "Yes" when I knew I wanted to say "No." Creating chaos by saying

"Yes" with hidden resentment (then repressing the resentment to feel chaotic).

Attaching myself to another person and then trying to control them as a way to create chaos.

Filling in for their shortcomings. Not allowing people to create their own chaos separately from myself.

Refusing to set boundaries in order to create the opportunity to be invaded. Creating a chaotic state of unrest.

If you would like to resume reading this material in the order it was intended, please return now to Study Guide, page 13 Parentification of Children

Clark, C. C. (2011). The art of healing. Retrieved May 10, 2011, from http://www.healthyplace.com/addictions/art-of-healing/adult-children-of-dysfunctional-families-alcoholism/menu-id-1074/

Appendix VIII
Basic Needs and Limits

My Needs (stable for the most part)
- Access to food, clean water, sanitation, clothing, shelter, and medical services.
- Income (for the first need) and the transportation to earn that income.
- Recovery and the income and transportation to maintain that recovery.
- School (education)
- Dreams
- To say I can choose.
- To say I love you.
- To say I'm sorry.
- To say I need you to help me meet my need.
- To know that the screw-ups I have are healthy.
- To hold and to be held.
- To have approval (in direct and non-controlling ways).
- To express (expulsion) my "self."
- To allow my "self" choices and the possibility of choices that are unknown.
- To set boundaries (and no explanation is necessary).
- To allow myself honesty.
- To say, "I don't know" when I don't know.
- To allow my honesty to be earned and not shared indiscriminately.
- To practice safe sex.
- To practice eating as needed and not in a way to stuff or over eat.
- To stop and clear myself when I'm in chaos or subtle diversion.

- To detach.
- To be separate in order to be close.
- To know that the best I can do is too much (controlling, approval seeking).
- Acknowledging when I'm hurt.
- Acknowledging when I'm sore.
- Acknowledging when my stomach hurts.

My Limits (at the time I have them)

- *The limits I have are not the same as the ability (I have) to do something.*
- *I'm unable to change the past.*
- *I'm unable to change the future by worrying about it.*
- *I have fears.*
- *I get tired.*
- *I'm unable to control what someone else is thinking of me.*
- *I'm unable to forcibly control someone else's actions without using destructive control behaviors. (to kill spirit)*
- *I can't control another person by being nice and accommodating.*

Asking for Needs to be Met

Asking for my needs to be met is more productive using the same non-victim role as with setting boundaries. As an infant, I had my own infant ways of asking for needs to be met. As an adult, I have adult ways to ask for my needs to be met. Clarity is important. Over-explaining the reason for my needs is control for approval's sake. I can choose not to control by explaining.

There is fear in asking for my needs to be met. My needs were shamed or discounted as a child. That fear of shaming or discounting generates hostility in my conversation style. The hostility is projected onto the listener. In return, they become hostile in order to protect themselves or become submissive in order to protect themselves. Either way, the listener will resent the interaction.

If you would like to resume reading this material in the order it was intended, please return now to Study Guide, page 22 Building Skills

Clark, C. C. (2011). The art of healing. Retrieved May 10, 2011, from http://www.healthyplace.com/addictions/art-of-healing/adult-children-of-dysfunctional-families-alcoholism/menu-id-1074/

Appendix IX

Emotions

Emotions add motivational coloring to cognitive processing and act as signals that direct us to notice and attend to particular cues. Emotions help us take adaptive action by calling attention to significant environmental events and stimuli. The emotional brain directs us toward experiences we seek and the cognitive brain tries to help us get there as intelligently as possible.

Traumatized people characteristically lose the capacity to draw upon emotions as guides for action. They might suffer from alexithymia, a disturbance in the ability to recognize and find words for emotions. They may be detached from their emotions, presenting with flat affect and complaining of a lack of interest and motivation in life and an inability to take action. Or their emotions may be experienced as urgent and immediate calls to action; the capacity to reflect on an emotion and allow it to be part of the data that guides action is lost and its expression becomes explosive and uncontrolled. Through nonverbal remembering triggered by reminders of the event, traumatized individuals relive the emotional tenor of previous traumatic experiences, finding themselves at the mercy of intense trauma-related emotions. These emotions can lead to impulsive, ineffective, conflicting, and irrational actions, such as lashing out physically or verbally, or feeling helpless, frozen, and numb. Emotional arousal in an individual with unresolved trauma thus often provokes action that is not an adaptive response to the present (nontraumatic) environment, but is more likely a version of an adaptive response to the original trauma.

Emotions usually follow a phasic pattern with a beginning, middle, and an end. However, for many traumatized individuals, the end never arrives. Emotional responses to very strong stimuli, such as trauma, do not appear to extinguish—a phenomenon that has been demonstrated in animal research by LeDoux, who noted that emotional memory may be forever. Traumatized individuals are often fixated on trauma-related emotions of grief, fear, terror, or anger. There might be a variety of reasons for this fixation; denial or lack of awareness of the connection between current emotions and past trauma; attempts to avoid more painful emotions; the inability to "think clearly"; or the inability to distinguish emotions from bodily sensations. Moreover, the emotions may relate to a variety of past events rather than only one. All these elements contribute to a circular, apparently never-ending reexperiencing of trauma-related emotions.

....emotions have two features: first, the internal sensation, which is "inwardly directed and private," and second, visible feature, which is "outwardly directed and public." Internal emotional states are thus experienced as subjective bodily sensations and are reflected in our outward presentation, giving signals to others around us about how we feel. Anger might be visible in the purse of the mouth, clenched fists, narrowed eyes, and general bodily tension. Fear may be communicated in hunched shoulders, held breath, and a pleading look in the eyes or in a bracing or moving away from the frightening stimulus. These bodily stances might be an immediate response to a current situation or a chronic, pervasive emotional state....In therapy we can utilize the outwardly directed physical manifestations to clarify, work with, and resolve trauma-related emotions. One client who presented with visible tension across her shoulders was directed to notice this tension and explore it for meaning. She reported that it felt like the tension was holding back anger— an insight gleaned from awareness of her body rather than from cognition. This insight led to the realization of an erroneous belief that she had no right to be angry at her abusive father. Working with the anger through the tension itself (slowly executing the movement the tension "wanted" to make, processing the associated memories, beliefs, and emotions, and learning to relax the tension) assisted this client on her road to fuller self-expression and resolution of the emotions related to her past traumatic events.

...when trauma-related emotions such as terror are coupled with body sensation, such as trembling, the client is encouraged to distinguish body sensations and movements from emotions. In these instances, we help clients differentiate emotional processing from sensorimotor processing. In our vernacular, emotional processing pertains to experiencing, articulating, and integrating emotions, whereas sensorimotor processing refers to experiencing, articulating, and integrating physical/sensory perception, body sensation, physiological arousal, and motor functioning. This differentiation between these two levels of processing is important in trauma therapy because clients often fail to discriminate between body sensations of arousal or movement and emotional feeling, which can lead to the escalation of both. This lack of discrimination is partly due to the fact that sensation and emotions occur simultaneously and suddenly, and partly because affect dysregulation and degrees of functional alexithymia are characteristic of posttrauma symptoms. Clients often find themselves struggling with the effects of overwhelming emotions, with little awareness of how the body participates in creating and sustaining these emotions.

If body sensations (e.g., trembling, rapid heart rate) are interpreted as an emotion (e.g., panic), each level of experience—sensorimotor and emotional—inflates and compounds the other....By working with the client to differentiate the sensation of physiological arousal from emotional arousal, the amount and kind of information are reduced and more ably processed by the client. Physiological arousal can be addressed, and often diminished, by uncoupling trauma-related emotion from body sensation through attending exclusively to the physical sensations of the arousal (without attributing meaning or emotion to them). Then, after the physiological arousal returns to a tolerable level, the client can look at the emotional contents of the traumatic experience and integrate both.

...traumatized people frequently experience themselves as being at the mercy of their sensations, physical and sensory reactions, as well as emotions, having lost the capacity to effectively regulate these functions. In the clinical practice of sensorimotor psychotherapy, we identify three general components of sensorimotor processing: inner-body sensation, five-sense perception, and movement.

Inner-Body Sensation: refers to the myriad of physical feelings that are continually created by movement of all sorts within the body. When a change occurs in the body, such as a hormonal shift or a muscular spasm, this change may be felt as an inner-body sensation. The contraction of the intestines, circulation of fluids, biochemical changes, the movements of breathing, or the movements of muscles, ligaments, or bones all cause inner-body sensations.

...movements occurring within our internal organs, such as racing of the heart, butterflies in the stomach, nausea, hunger, or that "gut feeling." We have a variety of nociceptors, most numerous in the skin and less numerous in tendons, joints, and organs, which relay various kinds of physical pain.

If you would like to resume reading this material in the order it was intended, please return now to Study Guide, page 28 Anatomy of an Emotion

Ogden, P, Minton, K. M., & Pain, C. (2006) Trauma and the body: A sensorimotor approach to psychotherapy (pp 11-15). New York: W.W. Norton & Company, Inc.

Appendix X

Conflict

You are a central delivery system for grace and truth in your spouse's life, and vice versa. You have a responsibility to both care for and confront one another. You are an agent for change and growth in each other. Love does not blind either of you to the other's problems; in fact, love demands that you pay attention to them so that you can help resolve them.

Who is better qualified to understand and speak to someone about a problem than the person who is living life right next to him? You are intimately involved with him. You see the real person, imperfections and all. His ways and actions affect you; you are not dispassionate about him. More than anyone, a spouse should be able to see what her partner's true problems are.

This idea, however, is foreign to some people. They have the notion that their spouse's job is to make them happy. Then when they are not happy, they think their spouse is not doing what he should be doing. In reality, nothing could be further from the truth. *Marriage is not about making each other happy; it is about growing and helping one's spouse to grow.* ...Happiness can and does come to a good marriage. Happiness, however, is a byproduct of growth and life. It is not the goal.[11]

---

[11] Cloud, H & Townsend, J. (2003). *Boundaries face to face: How to have that difficult conversation you've been avoiding* (pg 193).

Many of us live in two worlds when it comes to relationships. In one world we have friendly conversations in which we avoid all disagreements; in the other we have major conflict-type conversations that tear everybody and everything up. In the first world we have connection without truth, and in the second we have truth without connection.

Conversations work best when people both care for each other and tell the truth to each other. Good things happen. People get along, resolve issues, and still maintain the connection they need.

When people have had enough bad experiences in relationships, they begin avoiding conflict and confrontation altogether. They withdraw from truthful conversations. They fear the following things:

- **Losing the relationship:** They fear that the person will withdraw either physically or emotionally from them.

- **Being the object of anger:** they don't want to receive someone's rage or blame about being confronted.

- **Being hurtful:** They are concerned about wounding the person and hurting their feelings.

- **Being perceived as bad:** They want to be seen as a nice person and they fear they will be seen as unloving or unkind.[12]

Grand Rapids, MI: Zondervan.

If you would like to resume reading this material in the order it was intended, please return now to Study Guide, page 31

Guilt

---

[12] Cloud, H & Townsend, J. (2003). *Boundaries face to face: How to have that difficult conversation you've been avoiding* (pg 18-19). Grand Rapids, MI: Zondervan.

Appendix XI

Guilt

Many people without boundaries complain about how "so and so makes me feel guilty when I say no," as if the other person had some sort of power over them. This fantasy comes from childhood, when your parents seemed so powerful.

A part of you agrees with the message because it taps into strong parental messages in your emotional brain. And that is your problem; it is on your property, and you must gain control over it. See that being manipulated is your problem, and you will be able to master it.

1) Own the guilt.
2) Get into your support system.
3) Begin to examine where the guilt messages come from.
4) Become aware of your anger.
5) Forgive the controller
6) Set boundaries in practice situations with your supportive friends, then gradually set them in more difficult situations. This will help you to gain strength as well as gain the supportive "voices" you need to rework your conscience....new information that will become the new guiding structures in your head instead of the old voices.[13]

Acquire guilt. This may sound funny, but you are going to have to disobey your parental conscience to get well. You are

---

[13] Pg 271

going to have to do some things that are right but make you feel guilty. Do not let the guilt be your master any longer. Set the boundaries, and then get with your new supporters to let them help you with the guilt....You need the new connections to internalize new voices in your head. Do not be surprised by grief. This will be sad, but let others love you in that process. Mourners can be comforted.14

If you would like to resume reading this material in the order it was intended, please return now to Study Guide, page 32 Forgiveness

Cloud, H. & Townsend, J. (1992). Boundaries: When to say yes, how to say no to take control of your life (pp 271-2). Grand Rapids, MI: Zondervan.

---

14 Pg 272

Appendix XII

Forgiveness

"To err is human, to forgive is divine." And to not forgive is the most stupid thing we can do. Forgiveness is very hard. It means letting go of something that someone "owes" you. Forgiveness is freedom from the past; it is freedom from the abusive person who hurt you.15

The Bible compares forgiving people to releasing them from a legal debt. ...Attempts at collection may take many forms. You may try to please them to help them pay you back. You think that if you do a little something more, they will pay their bill and give you the love they owe....You think that if they just understood, they would make it better. They would pay what they owe....the problem is that things will get resolved in only one way: with grace and forgiveness. An eye for an eye and a tooth for a tooth does not work. The wrong can never be undone. But it can be forgiven and thereby rendered powerless.... To forgive means we will never get from that person what was owed us. And that is what we do not like, because that involves grieving for what will never be: The past will not be different. For some, this means grieving the childhood that never was. For others it means other things, but to hang on to the demand is to stay in unforgiveness, and that is the most destructive thing we can do to ourselves.16

---

15 Pg 267

16 Pg 268

Forgive. To not forgive is to lack boundaries. Unforgiving people allow other people to control them. Setting people who have hurt you free from an old debt is to stop wanting something from them; it sets you free as well…figure out what you want to do, set your course, and stick to it. Decide what your limits are, what you will allow yourself to be a party to, what you will no longer tolerate, and what consequences you will set.17

Forgiveness gives me boundaries because it unhooks me from the hurtful person, and then I can act responsibly, wisely. If I am not forgiving them, I am still in a destructive relationship with them. Gain grace from God, and let others' debts go. Do not keep seeking a bad account. Let it go, and go and get what you need from God and people who can give. That is a better life. Unforgiveness destroys boundaries. Forgiveness creates them, for it gets bad debt off of your property. Remember one last thing. Forgiveness is not denial. You must name the sin against you to forgive it.18

You may want to check out Clinton S. Clark's list of working definitions in Appendix XIII.

Cloud, H. & Townsend, J. (1992). Boundaries: When to say yes, how to say no to take control of your life. Grand Rapids, MI: Zondervan.

---

17 Pg 172

18 Pg 269

Appendix XIII

Working Definitions[19]

Definition: Abusive. To kill spirit or choice. To cause doubt. To cause self doubt. To abandon physically or emotionally. To threaten one's security. To corrode trust. To injure. To issue sadness or terror. To control without regard to boundary or well being.

Definition: Addict. A person who has acquired a set of dependency skills and is psychologically (or emotionally) restrained from operating independently without the use of compulsion or control.

Definition: Attached or Attached in an unhealthy way. The use of destructive control behaviors.

Definition: Attack. "To set upon forcefully. To assail with unfriendly or bitter words. To begin to affect. To set to work on. To make an onslaught on. A belligerent or antagonistic action. The beginning of destructive action" (Webster's New Collegiate Dictionary. G. & C. Merriam Co. 1973).

Definition: Bad Choices. Bad Choices are choices which were deemed as being less than perfect or uncomfortable by the addict parent. Includes:

- Taking care of myself.
- Not taking care of the addict parent's needs.

---

[19] Clark, C. C. (2011). *The art of healing*. Retrieved May 10, 2011, from http://www.healthyplace.com/addictions/art-of-healing/adult-children-of-dysfunctional-families-alcoholism/menu-id-1074/

- Not expecting myself to go beyond my age appropriate limits.
- Setting a boundary.
- Or any other choice (or action) that the addict deemed as being bad because of their negative or uncomfortable reaction to it.

Definition: Bad Feelings. Bad feelings are defined by the addict parent as the feelings which constitute emotional or physiological pain such as sadness, grief, fear, helplessness, anger, disappointment, anxiety, resentment, nervousness, frustration, guilt, loneliness, shame, or any other feelings of pain.

Definition: Beating. Intent to traumatize. Intent to inflict excessive force. To spank without boundary (lack of protection) such as removal of the child's clothing (bare skin contact) or to spank repeatedly or to spank out of control in a rage. Intent to inflict excessive pain by using an object to strike with such as boards or belts. To strike a body part other than the buttocks. To spank using closed hand. To vent without boundary.

Definition: Being needy. In need of something such as help, comfort, nurturing, emotional support, etc.

Definition: Blame. The projecting of responsibility for an opinion, action, behavior, or a feeling onto someone else.

Definition: Boundary Violation. A boundary violation is an invasion of one person by another without permission. A child whose boundaries are being invaded is being terrorized and coerced by the intruder.

Definition: Chaos. An inner turmoil process that allows me to maintain a level of terror that exceeds or matches the terror I experienced in childhood. A state of internal unrest.

Definition: Crazy Making Game. To begin to feel crazy or insane. To lack acknowledgement for a belief system. To have a support system that denies or filters information in a way to denounce feelings or intuition. To lack affirmation. To be attacked without confirmation. To begin to feel hyper vigilant or "on guard." To lose confidence or have trust destroyed.

Definition: Danger. Threat of invasion, intrusion, unexpected violence, catastrophe, shaming, humiliation, false guilt, killing of spirit, abuse, abandonment, restricting the right to flee, forced activity, compulsion, dependence, projection, death, injury, destructive control behaviors.

Definition: Demythification. To undo a myth. To change a belief system. To take off a pedestal. To announce flexibility. To examine.

Definition: Denial. To filter information in and out of memory in order to support an established belief system. To deny self. To deny self information to protect a perception or belief. To corrupt information and feedback. To corrupt feelings. To lack affirmation of another belief system. To unconsciously manipulate as a way to get a need met. To use in support of, i.e. to use the child as an emotional support system in order to maintain the addict parent's established belief system.

Definition: Destructive control behaviors. To control in a destructive way. To destroy spirit or consciousness. To deny or avoid. To distort a belief system. To control in an addictive or dependent way. To control without regard to boundary or consequence. To make like a drug in order to alter feeling or emotion.

Definition: Detachment or Detached. Non-controlling. Non-use of destructive control behaviors. The practice of a detachment skill.

Definition: Dysfunctional. To impair growth or development. To cause to remain hidden. Unexamined belief. To repeat without consideration. To lack listening or communication skills. To lack boundary or boundary setting skills.

Definition: Feedback. A response by the listener to what they've heard and understood the speaker to say. An intuitive response. A perception of what was said.

Definition: Fishing. "Fishing" is an indirect way of soliciting approval, acceptance, ok-ed-ness, or affirmation.

Definition: Hidden agenda. Hidden agendas are ulterior motives or hidden reasons. In this situation the agenda of using the child as emotional support to feel better is hidden and the presentation of themselves (the addict parent) as a concerned listener is shown.

Definition: Illusionary power. To imagine another to have a power. To place in authority. To render or renounce power or control. To unjustly place on a pedestal. To make infallible. To avoid responsibility.

Definition: Inanimate Object. To be without spirit. To be without choice or free will. To be immobile.

Definition: Invisible. To be without needs. To "Not speak until spoken to." To not need assistance or listening support. To be without (or silent about) pain, physically or emotionally. To be without complaint. To be without need for approval or affirmation. To be without expectation. To become limitless and without boundary. To be without age appropriate limitations.

Definition: Listen. To be in attendance of a conversation without the compulsion to control or participate. To align feelings with or in support of the speaker. To not divert or judge. Listening; The act of listening may include the asking of questions for clarification. The act of listening does not include feedback. Feedback is another separate part of communication other than listening.

Definition: Need. "a physiological or psychological requirement for the well-being of an organism" (Webster's New Collegiate Dictionary. G. & C. Merriam Co. 1973).

Definition: Being needy. In need of something from the addict parent, such as help, comfort, nurturing, emotional support, etc. May also describe the child's reaction to an addict parent.

Definition: Nice. To not complain. To let someone hurt me without speaking up. To endure something I can't stand without a word. To be in the company of someone I hate without report. To control my feelings. To conceal my feelings of being angry or frustrated. To use kindness as a way to approval seek in order to avoid disapproval or the possibility of being abused.

Definition: Personal protective space. A cushion of distance, physical or psychological, which protects a living organism's emotional or spiritual habitat within their physical body or protects their physical body within their environment from the perception of harm. The distance is uniquely defined by each individual organism in response to the perception of their safety at the time a threat is perceived. A part of the survival instinct mechanism.

Definition: Planned change. A program of recovery which is planned. Such as Counseling, 12 Step Meetings, In-patient treatment programs, Out-patient treatment programs.

Definition: Project. "to attribute (something in one's own mind) to a person, group, or object" (Webster's New Collegiate Dictionary. G. & C. Merriam Co. 1973).

Definition: Project. To transmit from the source to another place. To attack. To assign responsibility.

Definition: Rigid. Unyielding. Inflexible belief system to protect an ego absent or injured. A need to protect.

Definition: Silence. The lack of feedback. Absence of feedback or developmental information.

Definition: Survive. To continue. Continued existence. To belong. To be a part of. To not be cast out of. To avoid injury or insult. To avoid abuse. To avoid death. To avoid a terror. Includes the detachment (numbing) of feeling or the repression of emotion (emotionally unavailable).

Definition: Systematic. "marked by thoroughness and regularity" (Webster's New Collegiate Dictionary. G. & C. Merriam Co. 1973).

Definition: Teasing. Intent to injure. Intent to humiliate with the intent of injuring. Anger or resentment expressed in an inappropriate or unclear way. An attack.

Definition: Terrorhood. meaning the abusive life of childhood including addiction, incest, sexual abuse, spousefication, compulsion, physical abuse, emotional abuse, ritualistic abuse, neglect, abandonment, the use of destructive control behaviors and the training to be an object of addiction.

Definition: Terrorize. "1: to fill with terror or anxiety; scare 2: to coerce by threat or violence." (Webster's New Collegiate Dictionary. G. & C. Merriam Co. 1973).

Definition: Terrorize. To entrap. To threaten injury or survival. To invade without regard to boundary. To make unsafe. To threaten takeover.

Definition: Terrorism. "the systematic use of terror esp. as a means of coercion" (Webster's New Collegiate Dictionary. G. & C. Merriam Co. 1973).

Definition: Test. To share a brief amount of information to see if the listener is going to react in a non-nurturing, addictive, or controlling way to the sharing of that information.

Definition: Use or Used. To exploit without permission or coerce permission. To manipulate individual will by using control. To place into a double bind. A compulsion. A lack of concession.

Definition: Victim. A behavioral condition. To behave as a victim. To project a sense of injury and helplessness. To use guilt or shame as a way of controlling another person into meeting the needs of the person behaving as a victim. Includes: To ignore or abandon as a way to control. To use anger that is repressed or an appearance of depression or forlorn as a way to control. To rage from a victimstance or to become passively aggressive as a way to control. To blame. To create resentment within another person; as a result of forcing them (controlling them) into a circumstance of which was not of their own choosing, through the use of guilt, shame, or the threat of abandonment. -cont.: Victimstance or Victim-stance. A place to start from. A point to begin acting out the role of a victim. To operate from the standpoint of a victim. Operating in the role as a victim. Further characteristics may also include behavioral traits as listed in the DSM-III-R under 301.00 PPD, 301.20 SPD, 301.50 HPD, 301.81 NPD, 301.82 APD, and 301.60 DPD. Note: Victim as defined here is not the same as a "victim" of abuse. These are separate ideas, i.e. playing the role of a victim verses being the "victim" of abuse.

This concludes the Boundaries 101 Study Guide. I look

forward to seeing you in class!!

Clark, C. C. (2011). The art of healing. Retrieved May 10, 2011, from   http://www.healthyplace.com/addictions/art-of-healing/adult-children-of-dysfunctional-families-alcoholism/menu-id-1074/

About the Author

Toni Rahman, MSW, LCSW got her bachelor's in biopsychology at Southeast Missouri State University and her Master's in Social Work at University of Missouri—Columbia. Between her undergraduate and graduate programs, she spent five years in Bangladesh, where she lived with her Bengali extended family. She has since authored an autobiographical novel, *Tahole, The politics of love*, and continues to study and teach about boundaries in a clinical setting. As a Clinical Social Worker, she works to help survivors overcome the effects of trauma. Her passions include Eastern and indigenous healing practices, psychology, spirituality and gender issues, as well as issues of social and economic justice. She is passionate about exploring ways to support others in making profound shifts in their life experience. She is trained in CranioSacral Therapy, Chinese Five Element Theory, Positive Parenting, EMDR, Dream Interpretation, Quantum Touch, and Energy Balancing. She now has a private practice as a counselor, therapist, and mentor in Columbia, MO.

Feel free to e-mail Toni at toniarahman@hotmail.com if you are interested in attending the Boundaries 101 Course.